FLAVOR OVERLOAD

OVER 50 VEGAN COMFORT FOOD RECIPES

VOLUME 01

Easy Plant-Based Cookbook

PRESENTED BY FLY VEGAN

FLAVOR OVERLOAD

OVER 50 VEGAN COMFORT FOOD RECIPES

Volume 1

2018

By

Fly Vegan   E.J. Hunter

PRESENTED BY FLY VEGAN

FLAVOR OVERLOAD

OVER 50 VEGAN COMFORT FOOD RECIPES

VOLUME 01

PRESENTED BY FLY VEGAN

TABLE OF CONTENTS

The story behind Fly Vegan

I'm anxious to share all of the amazing flavors I've been able to cultivate. Cooking is my passion, what I enjoy more is teaching others how to execute a meal that brings joy to their whole family. My belief is once you develop a new way of thinking then you'll win every time. With this in mind, I thought, why can't we enjoy the same food we did before, only now in a vegan way? My fiancé, a New Orleans native taught me a thing or two about Creole and Cajun spices. I simply blended those flavors with my southern style and Fly Vegan was born. We've made it a mission to bring flavor to plant-based food. If you like southern foods, bold flavors and the feeling of nostalgia you get while enjoying a Plate of comfort food, try Fly Vegan Recipes.

If you're tired of throwing out recipes, you're in the right place.

We embrace the plant-based lifestyle as well as a healthy community. Welcome to tried and true plant based flavor overload. ENJOY!

"WHAT IS PLANT-BASED FOOD"

Pant-baed is a diet based on foods derived from plants, including vegetables, whole grains, nuts, seeds, legumes and fruits, but with few or no animal products. The use of the phrase has changed over time, and examples can be found of the phrase "plant-based diet" being used to refer to vegan diets, which contain no food from animal sources, to vegetarian diets which include eggs and dairy but no meat, and to diets with varying amounts of animal-based foods, such as semi-vegetarian diets which contain small amounts of meat.

BREAKFAST

JALAPEÑO CHEESE GRITS

Ingredients

1 cup vegan unsweetened milk

3 cups water

1 1/2 teaspoons kosher salt

1 cup stone ground grits

1/2 teaspoon freshly ground black pepper

1 tablespoons vegan butter

1 cup vegan cheese

1 1/2 cup of frozen corn

1 diced jalapeño

Number Of Servings:
6
Preparation Time:
30 min

Directions

Place the vegan milk, water, and salt into a large, heavy-bottomed pot over medium-high heat and bring to a boil. Once the milk mixture comes to a boil, gradually add the cornmeal while continually whisking. Once all of the grits have been incorporated, decrease the heat to low and cover.

Remove lid and whisk frequently, every 5 minutes, to prevent grits from sticking or forming lumps; make sure to get into corners of pot when whisking. Cook for 40 minutes or until mixture is creamy.

Remove from the heat, add the pepper and butter, corn, jalapeño and whisk to combine. Once the vegan butter is melted, gradually whisk in the cheese. Serve immediately.

Apple Sage Sausage

Ingredients
1 cup cooked brown rice
3⁄4cup rolled oats
2 tablespoons whole wheat flour
1 tablespoon ground flax seeds
1/4 cup applesauce
1 teaspoon liquid smoke
1 teaspoon molasses
2 tablespoons olive oil (divided)
2 tablespoons nutritional yeast
2 tablespoons tamari
1⁄2 teaspoon red pepper flakes
2 teaspoons Italian seasoning
1 teaspoon black pepper
1 1⁄2teaspoons ground sage

Directions
Stir together flax and water in a small bowl or cup, set aside.

in a food processor, add dry oats and pulse on high six or seven times, add the rice and pulse a few more times.

Add remaining ingredients including 1 Tablespoon oil and flax/water mixture and blend till just mixed. (do not over process, you can finish mixing together with your hands).

With dampened hands, form balls the size of a ping pong ball and then flatten into little patties about 1/4" thick (thicker if you like).

Coat the bottom of a non-stick frying pan with the remaining 1 tablespoon canola oil and heat over medium high.
When the oil is hot, cook the patties on each side until they are browned.
transfer to a paper towel to blot off any excess oil before serving.

Number Of Servings:
6
Preparation Time:
30 min

Banana Oat Pancakes

Ingredients
3/4 cup Old Fashioned Oats
2 medium Bananas, Mashed
1 1/2 cups Almond Milk
1 cup All-Purpose Flour
2 tablespoons Brown Sugar
1 1/2 teaspoons Baking Powder
1/2 teaspoon Salt
1/4 teaspoon Baking Soda
1 tablespoons Flaxseed meal+3
tablespoons of warm water
mixed
3 tablespoons Vegetable Oil
1/4 cup Chopped Pecans

Directions
In a medium bowl, mix together the oats, bananas, sugar, oil, milk and flax seed egg. Set them aside 5 min to soak and soften. Preheat a pancake griddle or skillet over medium high heat.

In a large bowl, whisk together the flour, baking powder, kosher salt, and baking soda. then pour the wet mixture into the dry. Stir until combined.

Butter the preheated surface and then pour the batter out about 1/4 cup at a time. Wait until the entire exposed surface is bubbly and the edges start to look golden brown.
Flip to cook the second side. Repeat with the remaining batter.

Number Of Servings:
4
Preparation Time:
30 minutes

Pecan Waffles

Ingredients

2 cups all-purpose flour

1/2 cup pecan pieces

2 tablespoons baking powder

1/4 teaspoon salt

1 flaxseed egg

1/4 cup sugar

1/2 cup apple sauce

1 teaspoon vanilla extract

1 cup melted vegan butter

2 1/2 cups almond milk

Vegetable oil for coating the waffle iron

1 cup pecan pieces

1/2 cup maple syrup

4 medium bananas, cut into 1/2-inch slices

Number Of Servings:

4

Preparation Time:

30 minutes

Directions

Preheat waffle iron and preheat the oven to 250 degrees F.

Combine the flour, pecans, baking powder and salt in a medium mixing bowl and whisk to combine. In another bowl, combine the flax egg, applesauce and sugar then whisk.
Add the vanilla extract, 1/2 cup melted vegan butter, and milk, and whisk together. Combine the wet mixture with the flour mixture and whisk until just combined.

Using a pastry brush, coat the waffle iron with some of the vegetable oil. Pour enough batter into the iron to just barely cover the waffle grid. Close the waffle iron and cook until golden brown, 4 to 6 minutes. Transfer to a baking sheet and keep warm in the oven while you prepare the remaining waffles.

In a salute pan, add 1/2 cup of vegan butter and pecan pieces. Cook, stirring occasionally, until pecan pieces are light golden, 2 to 3 minutes. Add the banana slices and cook until light golden and soft. Add the syrup and bring to a simmer. Serve with the warm waffles

Breakfast Casserole

Ingredients

1/2 cup bell pepper
1/2 cup onion
1 cup spinach
1 cup tomato
14oz extra firm tofu
1/2 cup vegan milk (almond)
1 teaspoon sea salt
1/2teaspoon black pepper
1 tsp garlic powder
1 tsp smoked paprika
2 tablespoon nutritional east
2 tablespoon cornstarch
2 tablespoon vegan cheese
1 tablespoon imitation bacon bits

Directions

Preheat oven to 375F/190C.

Heat olive oil over medium heat, and sauté onions and garlic until translucent. This should take about 2 minutes. Add tomatoes, spinach and cook until wilted.

In a blender, add tofu, nutritional yeast, cornstarch, vegan milk and seasonings. Blend the ingredients until you have a creamy consistency.

In a casserole dish combine the veggie mixture with the tofu mixture, spread evenly.

Bake in oven for 30 minutes, or until mixture is set.

Number Of Servings:
4
Preparation Time:
45 minutes

The Perfect Oatmeal

Ingredients

1 cup water
Pinch of salt
$1/2$ cup old-fashioned rolled oats
$1/2$ cup blueberries, fresh or frozen, thawed
1 tablespoon toasted chopped pecans
2 teaspoons pure maple syrup
1/4 teaspoon cinnamon

Directions

Bring water, cinnamon and salt to a boil in a small saucepan.

Stir in oats, then reduce heat to a medium low and allow the rolled oats to cook.

Stir occasionally until most of the liquid is absorbed. This will only take about 5 minutes.

Remove the oatmeal from the heat, cover and let it stand for a couple of minutes.
Add maple syrup and top with fresh blueberries and a of sweet pecans.

Bam! Breakfast is served. Serve with your favorite juice or smoothie.

Number Of Servings:
1
Preparation Time:
10 minutes

Fluffy Pancakes

Ingredients
1/2 cup applesauce
1 flaxseed egg
2 cups almond milk
2 cups flour
1 tablespoon baking powder
1/2 teaspoon salt
1 tablespoon sugar
1 1/2 teaspoon vanilla
2 teaspoon oil

Directions
In a large bowl, add flour, salt and baking powder, mix.

Add applesauce, flaxseed egg, vanilla, sugar, oil and almond milk and combine all of the mixture until smooth.

Heat a nonstick pan or griddle and spray with oil to lightly grease. Carefully pour 1/4 cup of batter onto the pan and into a circle and cook approximately 3-4 min.

When the bubbles on the surface of the batter burst, this means the pancake is ready to flip. Use a spatula to turn pancakes and cook until golden, making sure the middle is not doughy. Repeat the process with the remaining batter.

Number Of Servings:
4
Preparation Time:
30 minutes

APPETIZERS

Mac and Cheese Bites

Ingredients

6oz. pasta
1 cup vegan sour cream
1& 1/2 cup vegan cheese
1 teaspoon basil
1 teaspoon garlic powder
1 teaspoon smoked paprika
1 teaspoon sea salt
1/2 teaspoon crushed red pepper

Wet dredge
3/4 cup coconut milk
2 tablespoons flour

2 cups bread crumbs

Number Of Servings:
10
Preparation Time:
3 hours

Directions

Bring a large pot of lightly salted water to a boil. Add macaroni and cook per package directions; drain.

Meanwhile, melt sour cream and vegan cheese over medium heat, cooking until smooth then add seasoning,
Bring to a simmer and cook 2 minutes. Remove from heat.

Fold macaroni into sauce till mixed completely. Spread mac and cheese onto cookie sheet. Refrigerate at least 2 hours.

Use a scoop to spoon out about 1/4 cup of the mixture at a time and shape into 2 to 3 inch balls, compressing slightly.
Whisk coconut milk and flour together. Dip balls in flour mixture, then coat in panko breadcrumbs.

Heat oil in a deep 4-quart pot to 360 degrees on a deep-fry thermometer. Fry mac and cheese bites 3 to 4 minutes, until golden. Place on paper towels to drain, Serve immediately.

Chili Cheese Fries

Ingredients

Chili

1/2 cup onion

1/2 cup poblano peppers

2 cups fresh tomatoes

1 can rinsed and drained light kidney beans

1 pack chili seasoning

1 1/2 cup water

Fries

2 russet potatoes

1 teaspoon sea salt

1 teaspoon smoked paprika

1 teaspoon parsley

1 tablespoon garlic powder

1/2 teaspoon cayenne pepper

1 teaspoon olive oil

2 cups Vegan Cheese (So Delicious)

Number Of Servings:
2-3
Preparation Time:
1 hour

Directions

Melt vegan butter in the pan with onion and poblano peppers, sauté five minutes and add fresh tomato.

sauté until tomatoes break down takes about 10 min. Add kidney beans and pack of chili season and stir to combine. Add water cover and cook for 30 min. Stir often so it doesn't stick.

Prepare fries using a sharp knife slice a 1/4-inch piece off the potato lengthwise. This will give you a stable base to slice on. Rest the potato, cut side down, and slice potato into 1/4 to 3/8-inch planks. Stack planks in piles 2 to 3 planks high, and slice lengthwise into 1/4 to 3/8-inch strips. And... you just cut French fries!!

Add olive oil into a bowl with potatoes and seasoning, mix together. Place a cooling rack on top of baking sheet, place fries in a single layer on the cooling rack then place fries in the oven for forty minutes 400 degrees

Melt vegan cheese, using the double boiler method if it gets to thick, add 1 tbsp. coconut milk to thin it out Add chili on top of hot fries, then drizzle So Delicious Vegan Cheese on top. Pile on the hot peppers and vegan sour cream is a great addition as well.

Fried Green Tomatoes

Ingredients
3 green tomatoes

Wet dredge
1/2 cup un-sweet vegan milk
1 tablespoons unbleached flour

Dry dredge
Cornmeal (self-rising)1 teaspoon
old bay seasoning
1 teaspoon salt
1 teaspoon cayenne pepper
1 teaspoon basil
1 teaspoon thyme
1 teaspoon smoked paprika
1 teaspoon garlic powder
2 cups of oil to fry

Number Of Servings:
4-6
Preparation Time:
1 hour

Directions
Cut each tomato into 1/4in slices.

In a medium bowl, combine the cornmeal and seasoning, mix well. In a small bowl add flour and vegan milk and mix well.

Dredge each tomato in wet dredge, then dredge in the dry cornmeal mixture. Dip the tomatoes in wet dredge once again, covering both sides of each tomato in the cornmeal mixture one last time.

Heat the oil in a large sauté pan and fry the battered tomato slices over medium-high heat until they are golden brown on both sides. Remove from pan and drain the fried green tomatoes on a paper towel. Plate and serve.

Jalapeno Poppers

Ingredients
4 large jalapeño
3/4 cup vegan cream cheese
1/2 cup vegan cheese
1/3 cup imitation bacon bits
1 can of crescent dough

Directions
Preheat oven to 400 degrees F (204 C) and prep your jalapeños, splitting each in half and removing the seeds. Place peppers on baking sheet bake 375 for 30 minutes.

Combine vegan cheese, cream cheese and bacon bitsand mix evenly.

Fill each pepper half with the cheese mixture a then wrap each pepper with croissant dough, bake them for 12 minutes until they are a golden brown.

Number Of Servings:
4-6
Preparation Time:
1 hour

Parmesan Zucchini Chips (Gluten Free)

Ingredients
1 large zucchini

Crumb Coat
2-1/2 cup corn flakes

3 tablespoon vegan parmesan cheese
1 tablespoon parsley flakes

Wet Coat
1 cup almond milk
1/3 cup gluten free flour
1 teaspoon garlic powder
1 teaspoon smoked paprika
1 teaspoon sea salt
1 teaspoon black pepper

Ranch Dipping Sauce
1/3 cup vegan mayo
1 teaspoon basil
1 teaspoon parsley
1 teaspoon garlic powder
1/2 teaspoon pepper

Number Of Servings:
4-6
Preparation Time:
1 hour

Directions
Preheat oven to 400 degrees. Wash and slice zucchini so they are 1/4-inch thick or so. In a bowl add dried parsley, cornflakes and Parmesan cheese.

Process for about 45 seconds in blender to make crumbs. Next, prepare the wet dredge, include dry seasonings.
Spoon in flour, garlic, paprika, sea salt, black pepper and mix together.

Grab zucchini and put in wet dredge and then add to dry dredge. Repeat with the remaining slices. Place on baking sheet lined with parchment paper.

Cooking times sometimes vary, but generally you should bake until crisp. Normal cooking times are approximately 20-30 minutes after putting them into the oven. When they are ready, remove from baking sheet. Plate and serve with dipping sauce.

Southwest Egg Roll

Ingredients

Egg Rolls
1/2 onion
1/2 bell pepper
1 cup corn
1&1/2 cup black beans
3 cups Spinach
1 cup vegan cheese(Daiya)
1 teaspoons cumin
1 teaspoon red pepper flakes
1 tablespoon garlic powder
1 teaspoon sea salt
1 teaspoon chili powder
8 flour tortilla

Southwest Dip
1/2 cup mayo
1 tablespoon lime juice
2 tablespoon cilantro
1 tablespoon sriracha
1/2 teaspoon salt
1/2 teaspoon pepper

Number Of Servings:
8
Preparation Time:
1 hour

Directions

In a large skillet, add a bit of vegetable oil. Sauté the bell peppers and onions over medium high heat for 5 minutes. They should be translucent.

Add the corn, black beans, spinach, red pepper flakes, cumin, chili powder, salt, and cayenne pepper to the skillet. Make sure everything is combined; continue to cook for about 10 minutes then turn off the heat. Add the vegan cheese now and stir until the cheese melts.

Spoon in 1/4 cup of the filling into the center of a tortilla. Fold each end, tightly roll the tortilla burrito style. Let it reston the seam. Repeat this process with the remainder of the tortillas and filling. Cover with plastic wrap and freeze for at least 4 hours.

While the egg rolls are freezing, make the southwest dip. Combine the ingredients into a bowl and mix them till smooth. Refrigerate the sauce until egg rolls are ready to serve.

Remove the egg rolls from the freezer and heat the oil. Deep-fry the stuffed egg rolls in hot oil until they become golden brown and move them to a paper towel lined container to drain. Plate them along with the sauce and enjoy as a snack or appetizer.

SOUP & SALAD

Potato Salad

Ingredients

2 pounds of red potatoes diced
2 tablespoon mustard
1/4 cup relish
1/2 cup vegan mayo
1/2 cup diced
red bell pepper
1/2 cup diced red onion
1/2 cup firm dice tofu (Boiled egg replacement)
1 tablespoon basil
1 tablespoon garlic powder
1 tablespoon smoked paprika
1 teaspoon sea salt

Number Of Servings:
4-6
Preparation Time:
30 min

Directions

Start by boiling the red potatoes, place diced potatoes in a large pot fill pot till the potatoes are covered with water. Cover and boil 15 minutes or until tender. Drain and chill potatoes till cool to touch.

In a large bowl, combine potatoes, mustard, tofu, mayo, basil, garlic powder, paprika, bell pepper, relish and onion. Mix all the ingredients, tossing gently to coat. Be careful not to mash the potatoes.

Cover and refrigerate for a couple of hours. Serve, it's the perfect side dish.

Macaroni and Tuna-less Salad

Ingredients
4 oz macaroni elbows
2 tablespoon sweet salad cubes
1 teaspoon maple syrup
2 tablespoon dijon mustard
1 tablespoon apple cider vinegar
1/2 cup onion
1/2 cup bell Pepper
1 teaspoon kelp or dulse
seaweed flakes
1 teaspoon smoked paprika
1 & 1/2 teaspoon sea salt
1 teaspoon basil
1 Can of garbanzo beans
1/3 cup vegan mayo

Directions
Cook pasta according to package when done. Drain & set aside.

In a large bowl, add garbanzo beans mash the beans to make them a more paste like texture. this can also be done in a food processor.

Add the seasoning, seaweed, bell pepper, onion, relish, syrup, vinegar and tofu. Stir to combine.

Stir in pasta. Garnish with paprika. Refrigerate for at least 2 hours.

Number Of Servings:
4
Preparation Time:
30 minutes

Spaghetti Salad Recipe

Ingredients

1 8oz box of spaghetti
1 cucumber
1 tomato
1/2 cup red onion
4oz black olives
1 tablespoon garlic powder
1 tablespoon smoked paprika
1 tablespoon parsley
1 tablespoon basil
1 teaspoon crushed red pepper
1 teaspoon sea salt
1/4 cup balsamic vinegar
1 bottle Italian dressing

Directions

Dice the cucumber, tomato and the red onion. Add them to a bowl with the black olives.

Add in seasonings, zesty Italian dressing and balsamic vinegar. Mix, Let them marinate in the refridgeretor for about 30 minutes.

In a large pot, start the pasta and cook as directed. Drain and cool.

Next, add the pasta to the bowl with the vegetable mixture and combine. Don't forget to take a picture and share.

Number Of Servings:
6-8
Preparation Time:
40 minutes

Vegan Cobb Salad

Ingredients

Salad

1 head Romaine lettuce, roughly chopped

1 1/2 cups diced tomatoes

1 cup diced cucumber

8 slices tempeh bacon cooked and crumbled

1 red onion finely sliced

1 avocado cubed

1 cup firm tofu diced (optional)

Vegan Blue Cheese Dressing

1 teaspoon Agave Nectar

2 tablespoons lemon juice

1/2 cup mayonnaise

3 tbsp almond milk or cashew milk

2 tablespoons Tahini

1 tsp garlic powder

¼ teaspoon sea salt

2 tablespoons parsley

Directions

Salad assembly

Simply add Romaine lettuce to a large serving tray. Form rows of each ingredient. Assemble chopped tofu, diced tomatoes, diced avocado, diced cucumber, red onions, and crumbled tempeh bacon.

Vegan Blue Cheese Dressing

Gather all of the ingredients for the dressing and place in a bowl. Whisk together till smooth and chill.

Number Of Servings:
4
Preparation Time:
20 minutes

Gazpacho Salad

Ingredients

1/2 cup red onion, diced
2 cloves garlic, minced
1 teaspoon Dijon mustard
1 teaspoon basil
1 teaspoon of thyme
1 tablespoon apple cider vinegar
1/3 cup extra-virgin olive oil
2 cups tomatoes
1 yellow bell pepper diced
1 cucumber, peeled and cubed
2 slices sour dough bread, crusts removed

Directions

To make the Gazpacho salad, start by adding garlic into a small bowl. Whisk in the mustard and vinegar. Now, add olive oil in a steady stream, continue to whisk until emulsified, then add seasoning.

Add fresh red tomatoes, peppers, cucumbers, and onions in a bowl. Mix them together.

Next, toast the sour dough bread, and cut into cubes. Sprinkle over salad, drizzle with the succulent vinaigrette dressing.

Number Of Servings:
4
Preparation Time:
20 minutes

Gumbo

Ingredients

1/2 cup oil
1 cup flour
2 cups chopped tomatoes
3 minced cloves of garlic
1 cup of chopped bell pepper
2 cups of chopped onion
1 cup of chopped celery
1 tablespoon garlic powder
1 tablespoon onion powder
1 tablespoon basil
1 tablespoon thyme
1 tablespoon smoked paprika
1 tablespoon cayenne
1 teaspoon gumbo file
2 teaspoon sea salt
3 bay leaves
1 tablespoon Better than Bouillon
10 cups of water
2 cup chopped okra
1 vegan shrimp(king prawn shrimp)
2 vegan sausages sliced (field roast)

Number Of Servings:
2
Preparation Time:
2 hours

Directions

Combine the oil and flour in a large Dutch oven over medium heat. Stir slowly and constantly for 10-15 minutes, making a dark brown roux. You'll know if you're doing it right, the color should look like a penny.

Add the onion, celery, garlic, tomatoes, and bell pepper. Continue to stir for 4 to 5 minutes until onion are translucent.

Add the seasonings, Better than Bouillon and bay leaves. Continue to stir for 3 to 4 minutes. Next, add water. Stir until the roux mixture and water are well combined.

Bring to a boil, then reduce heat to medium-low. Cook uncovered for about one hour, stirring occasionally.

Now, add the okra into the Dutch oven and allow it to cook for 30 more minutes.

In a pan, add the sliced sausage on medium high heat, cook till brown on each side.

Stir in the vegan sausages and vegan shrimp. Remove the bay leaves and serve in deep bowls over, white rice.

Vegetable Stew

Ingredients
1 tablespoon olive oil
1 cup chopped onion
1 cup chopped bell pepper
1 cup chopped celery
3 minced cloves of garlic
1 cup chopped tomato
8 cups of water
1 tablespoon Better than bouillon
1 tablespoon thyme
1 tablespoon basil
1 tablespoon sea salt
1 teaspoon crushed red pepper
1 tablespoon smoked paprika
2 pounds of potatoes
1 cup copped carrots
1 cup sweet peas
1 cup Mushroom
2 tablespoon Cornstarch mixed
with ½ cup of water

Number Of Servings:
4-6
Preparation Time:
1 hour

Directions
Heat oil in a large, saucepan over medium heat. Add onions, garlic, bell pepper, celery, and mushrooms. Cook 10 minutes, stirring frequently.

Add the potatoes, carrots, sweet peas and tomatoes. Add the Better than bouillon along with the seasonings, fill the pot with water then add cornstarch mixture.

Cover and simmer 45 minutes, or until vegetables are tender. Stir occasionally while cooking.

Ingredients

1/2 cup vegan butter
1 cup all-purpose flour
2 cups organic sugar, divided
1 tablespoon baking powder
¼ teaspoon salt
1 cup coconut milk
5 cups fresh diced apple slices
1 tablespoon lemon juice
1 teaspoon vanilla extract
1 teaspoon ground cinnamon

Number Of Servings:
6
Preparation Time:
1 Hour

Directions

Melt butter in a 13- x 9-inch baking dish.

Combine flour, 1 cup of sugar, baking powder, and salt; add milk, stirring just until dry ingredients are moistened. Pour batter over butter.

Bring remaining the 1 cup organic sugar, apple slices, and lemon juice to a boil over medium-high heat. Let this cook for 10 minutes, stirring constantly.

Pour over batter, do not stir. Sprinkle the top with a little cinnamon and sugar.
Bake at 375° for 40 to 45 minutes or until golden brown, Serve cobbler warm, a scoop of vanilla ice cream is a great addition.

Ingredients

1/4 cup vegan butter
1 cup brown sugar
1 tsp cinnamon
3-4 bananas
1/2 cup dark rum
1 paint vegan vanilla ice cream

Directions

Melt the butter in a large skillet over medium heat. Add the brown sugar, cinnamon and cook, stirring, until the sugar dissolves, about 2 minutes.

Add the bananas and cook until the bananas start to soften and brown, about 3 minutes. Carefully add the rum and shake the pan back and forth to warm the rum and flame the pan. (Or, off the heat, carefully ignite the pan with a match.) Shake the pan back and forth, basting the bananas, until the flame dies.

Serve the bananas with a scoop of vegan ice cream.

Number Of Servings:
4
Preparation Time:
20 minutes

Ingredients

Dough
2 cups all-purpose flour
1 tablespoon baking powder
1 cup fresh blueberries
1/2 teaspoon salt
2 tablespoons sugar
5 tablespoons vegan butter, frozen,
cut in chunks
1 cup coconut milk

Glaze
1/3 cup lemon juice
2 cups powder sugar, sifted
1 tablespoon vegan butter
1 lemon, zest finely grated

Number Of Servings:
8
Preparation Time:
1 Hour

Directions

Pre heat the oven 375°FH

Combine the flour, baking powder,
salt, and sugar.
Cut in the frozen vegan butter coating
the pieces with the flour. The mixture
should look like coarse crumbs.

Fold the blueberries into the batter. Be
careful not mash the blueberries.
Their strong color will bleed into the
dough. Make a well in the center and
pour in the heavy cream. Next, fold
everything together but do not
overwork the dough.

Roll the dough out on a lightly floured
surface into a rectangle about 12 by 3
by 1 1/4 inches. Cut the rectangle in
half, then cut the pieces in half one
more time, giving you 4 (3-inch)
squares. Next, cut the squares in half
but diagonally. This will give it the
classic triangle shape.

Place the scones on an un-greased
cookie sheet and brush the top of the
scones with coconut milk. Bake for 15
to 20 minutes or until golden brown.
Let the scones cool.

In a glass bowl, mix the lemon juice
with the powder sugar until dissolved.
Place bowl over a pot of simmering
water for the double-boiler method.
Whisk in the butter and lemon zest
and continue whisking in the double
boiler till it's smooth.

Drizzle the lemon glaze over the
scones. Now stand back and look at
your work. You did it!

Ingredients

Cake

2 cups flour

2 tablespoon coco powder

1 teaspoon baking soda and

1/2 teaspoon salt

1 1/2 cups sugar

1 1/2 oil

1/2 cup apple sauce

1 tablespoon flax seed meal

1 teaspoon vinegar

2 teaspoon vanilla

1/2 cup melted chocolate

Icing

4 cups powered sugar

3/4 cup vegetable shortening

1/2 cup cashew milk

1 tsp almond flavor

Number Of Servings:
10
Preparation Time:
1 Hour

Directions

To Make the Cake: Preheat your oven to 350F (180C). Prepare two 8" round baking tins by lightly greasing them, and then cutting a circle of parchment paper to fit into the bottom.

In a large bowl whisk together all of the dry ingredients, then set aside.

In a medium bowl whisk together all of the wet ingredients. Pour the wet ingredients into the dry ingredients and mix until just combined. Don't over mix. Divide the batter into the prepared pans, then pop them in the oven. Bake for about 40 minutes until a toothpick inserted into the center comes out clean. Let the cakes cool completely before frosting.

Frosting: Use a mixer to blend all of the frosting ingredients except for the non-dairy milk. Blend until whipped and creamy. If the frosting is a bit too stiff, add 1 to 2 tablespoons of non-dairy milk as needed until desired consistency is reached.

Assemble the Cake: Run a knife around the edges of the cake pans, and flip the pans over to remove the cakes. Remove the parchment paper and discard. Place the first cake on your cake plate, and spread about half of the frosting on top. Place the second cake on top of the frosted cake, and spread the remaining frosting on top of that cake. Add swirl patterns with your spatula to make it pretty. Store the cake in the fridge or a cool place until you are ready to serve.

Ingredients

1 cup sugar
1 cup brown sugar
3/4 cups vegan butter
1/3 cup applesauce
1 Flaxseed egg =1 tbsp. flaxseed
meal+3 tbsp. warm water
1 teaspoon vanilla
2 cups flour
1/2 teaspoon salt
1 teaspoon baking powder
1/2tsp baking soda
1 cup of chocolate chips

Number Of Servings:
18
Preparation Time:
30 minutes

Directions

Preheat oven to 350.

In a small bowl, combine flax meal and warm water. Allow to sit and gel for about 5 minutes.

Using a larger bowl, mix butter and both sugars until light and creamy. Add vanilla extract, applesauce flax meal mixture. Mix well.

Next, add in baking powder, baking soda, flour, and salt. Stir to combine ingredients. Now, add the chocolate chips.

Roll 1-inch balls onto a lined baking sheet and bake for 12 minutes. Remove from the oven and allow cookies to cool. It may be a good idea to put them out of reach. These chocolate chip cookies are a great idea for your kid classroom parties and sleepover events. Makes 36 cookies.

Ingredients

3 cups all-purpose flour

2 cups cane sugar

1 teaspoon baking soda

1 teaspoon baking powder

1 teaspoon sea salt

1 teaspoon ground cinnamon

2 cups diced ripe bananas (about 3 medium)

1/2 cup coconut flakes

2 tablespoons flaxseed meal

1/2 cup chopped toasted pecans

3/4 cup vegetable oil

1 cup can crushed pineapple, undrained

2 teaspoons vanilla extract

Glaze

1/4 cup vegan cream cheese

1/4 cup vegan butter

2 cups of powder sugar

1 teaspoon vanilla extract

1 tablespoon coconut milk

Number Of Servings:
18
Preparation Time:
30 minutes

Directions

Prepare a Bundt pan by greasing and flouring or use cooking spray. Preheat oven to 350 degrees F.

In a large bowl, combine flour, baking soda, cinnamon, and salt. Stir in flaxseed eggs, mashed bananas, pineapple, oil, sugar and vanilla. Mix until dry ingredients are moistened. Pour batter into bundt pan.

Bake in preheated oven for 60 to 70 minutes or until cake tests done. Cool cake in pan on wire rack for 15 minutes; remove from pan to wire rack and cool completely.

To prepare glaze: In the bowl of a food processor, combine the vegan cream cheese, powdered sugar, vanilla, and 1 tablespoon coconut milk until well blended and smooth. Add the remaining milk 1 teaspoon at a time if needed for glaze consistency. Pour glaze over cooled cake, then sprinkle with pecans.

Ingredients

1/2 cup vegan butter
1 cup peanut butter
1 cup brown sugar
1 cup sugar
1/2 cup applesauce
2 teaspoons vanilla extract
1 teaspoon almond extract
2 1/4 cup unbleached flour
1/2 teaspoon baking soda
1 teaspoon salt
1 tablespoon coconut milk

Number Of Servings:
18
Preparation Time:
30 minutes

Directions

Preheat oven to 375 degrees In a large mixing bowl, cream together the peanut butter, brown & white sugar for 1 minute. Add in the applesauce, vanilla & almond extract then beat for another 30 seconds.

In a separate mixing bowl, mix the dry ingredients together flour, baking powder, baking soda, and salt. While beating the peanut butter mixture, add in the flour mixture and beat until dough forms.

Add milk and continue to beat until distributed. Line two baking sheets with parchment paper. Roll the dough into balls (about 1½tablespoons per cookie), drop on cookie sheet, and flatten with a fork one way and then the other to create a crisscross pattern.

Bake for 8-9 minutes tops until just starting to turn golden on edges .place on wire rack till completely cool. Enjoy!

MAIN COURSES

Cajun Pasta

Ingredients

1 16oz box of Rigatoni pasta
2 tablespoon vegan butter
1&1/2 cup onion
1 cup celery
6oz fresh spinach
1 cup bell pepper
2 cup mushroom
2 cups grape tomato
1 tablespoon Better than bouillon paste or bouillon cube
1 tablespoon basil
1 tablespoon thyme
1 tablespoon smoked paprika
1 tablespoon garlic powder
1 tablespoon onion powder
1/2 teaspoon sea salt
1 teaspoon cayenne pepper

Number Of Servings:
6-8
Preparation Time:
30 min

Directions

Heat a large skillet on medium-high heat. Place in the vegan butter and heat until melted. Add minced garlic, bell pepper, celery and onion. Let it cook for about five minutes.

Add mushrooms, fresh chopped tomatoes, spinach, and seasoning. Mix well and continue cooking for about 15 minutes.

Cook pasta according to package instructions. Drain to prevent pasta from over cooking.

Add your pasta to the skillet with the vegetables mixture. Mix well. Your pasta is now ready to serve. Enjoy!

Cajun Fried Nuggets

Ingredients

1 can young jackfruit in brine or water
½ tsp Better Than Bouillon

dry dredge
1 cup Flour
2 teaspoons salt
1/2 teaspoon black pepper
1 teaspoon onion powder
1 teaspoon garlic powder
1 teaspoon smoked paprika
1 teaspoon thyme
1 basil
1/4 cayenne pepper

wet dredge
1/2 cup Vegan sour cream
2 tablespoons almond milk
3 tablespoons Louisiana Hot Sauce

Number Of Servings:
2
Preparation Time:
30 min

Directions

Rinse and drain the jackfruit, place into a bowl. Add Better Than Bouillon, coconut milk and hot sauce. Combine mixture and marinate jackfruit for one hour.

In a bowl, make a dry dredge by combining flour and seasoning.

In a separate bowl, place the vegan sour cream, hot sauce, and milk.

Dip one piece of jackfruit into the vegan sour cream mixture, then coat it with the flour mixture. Dip the jackfruit back into the wet dredge and then back the dry dredge. repeat steps with remaining peaces of jackfruit.

Heat oil in a skillet on medium high heat (you need enough oil to cover the bottom of the pan about 1 inch.) Place jackfruit in the oil, being careful not to splash the oil. Cooking each piece 3 minutes on each side or until golden brown. Transfer each piece to a plate lined with paper towels.

Cajun Rice

Ingredients

2 cups chopped onion
1-1/2 cups chopped bell pepper
1 cup chopped celery
1 cup sliced mushroom
4 cloves garlic minced
1 tablespoon vegan butter
1 tablespoons better than bouillon paste
3 bay leaves
1 tablespoon Smoked Paprika
1 tablespoon Sea Salt
1 teaspoon Cayenne pepper
1 tablespoon Thyme
1 tablespoon Basil
3 cups Par Boiled Rice
2 cups Beef-less Crumbles
6 cups Water
1/4 cup Soy Sauce

Number Of Servings:
6
Preparation Time:
45 min

Directions

In a large pot, heat the vegan butter over medium heat.

Add the butter, onions, bell peppers, garlic, celery and sauté the vegetables until tender and lightly caramelized, 10 minutes.

Add the beef-less crumbles & mushroom, using the spoon to break the beef-less crumbles into small pieces, cook until mushrooms are tender, 5 minutes.

Add better than bouillon, bay leaves, thyme, salt, paprika, basil, soy sauce, cayenne and cook until the spices are fragrant, 2 to 3 minutes.

Add the par-boiled rice and water stirring, until well combined. Cover pot with a lid. Cook rice for 25 min. Remove lid take out the bay leaves, use a fork to fluff the rice.

Cajun Twice Baked Potatoes

Ingredients

4 large baking potatoes, about 1
pound each
1 tablespoon olive oil
1/2 tablespoon sea salt
1/2 teaspoon ground white pepper
1 teaspoon smoked paprika 1
tablespoon garlic powder
1/2 teaspoon thyme
1/2 teaspoon basil
3 tablespoons imitation bacon bits
1/4 cup nutritional yeast
1 cup vegan sour cream
4 tablespoons vegan butter
3 tablespoons almond milk or
cashew milk
2 tablespoons chopped fresh chives
2 cups vegan cheese (So Delicious)

Number Of Servings:
4
Preparation Time:
2 hours

Directions

Preheat oven to 400° degrees FH.
Line a large baking sheet with
parchment paper; set aside.

Rub potatoes with oil and season
with 1/2 teaspoon salt and 1/8
teaspoon black pepper.

Place on prepared baking sheet and
bake until fork-tender for 1 hour to 1
hour and 30 minutes.

Remove from oven and let stand
until cool enough to handle.

Peel one potato; discard skin and
place pulp in a large bowl. Cut the
top quarter from each of the
remaining 4 potatoes.
Using a spoon, scoop pulp from
potatoes into bowl leaving a 1/4-inch
layer of pulp around the skin.
Return potato shells to baking sheet.

Using a mixer, whip potatoes until
smooth. Add sour cream, milk,
butter, bacon bits, chives and
seasoning; mix with spoon until
everything is incorporated.

Spoon potato mixture back into
potato shells, top with cheese and
bake at 375 degrees until potatoes
are hot and cheese is melted, about
15 minutes.
Enjoy.

Easy Veggie Stir-fry

Ingredients

3 tablespoons olive oil
1 cup diced eggplant
1 cup chopped fresh tomatoes
1/2 cup chopped onions
1/2 cup diced yellow squash
1/2 cup diced zucchini
1/2 cup fresh whole kernel corn
(from 1 ear of corn)
1/4 cup chopped fresh basil
4 cloves garlic minced
1 teaspoon salt, or more to taste
1/4 teaspoon ground black
pepper

Directions

Heat the oil in a large skillet over medium-high heat. Add the remaining ingredients, and stir-fry, stirring constantly, for 5 to 6 minutes, or until tender.

Serve, with cooked rice.

Number Of Servings:
2
Preparation Time:
20 minutes

Holiday Ham (Seitan)

Ingredients

Dough
2 cups vital wheat gluten
2 tablespoon of garbanzo bean flour
1 tablespoon smoked paprika
1 teaspoon garlic powder
1 teaspoon onion powder
1/4 teaspoon salt
1 teaspoon Vegetable base
2 teaspoon Liquid smoke
1 tablespoon Beet juice
1 tablespoon Maple syrup
1-1/2 cup Water
2 teaspoon Olive oil

Number Of Servings:
2
Preparation Time:
20 minutes

Directions

in a large bowl, combine Seitan dry ingredients using a whisk. You'll need to create a well in the center of the bowl.

Next, add wet ingredients. Mix them through until they are combined, kneed for about 5 minutes.

Form ingredients into a ball and place in steamer for 45 minutes. Flip the dough at the 30 minute mark.

While the Seitan is steaming, place all of the ingredients for the glaze in a bowl and mix them together.

Remove Seitan from steamer and place in baking dish. Turn the oven on and preheat to 200 degrees Celsius or 390 degrees Fahrenheit.

Mark the "ham" in a crisscross pattern and place cloves in the center of the squares you masterfully created. Pour glaze over the ham so it is completely covered. Bake for 15 minutes.

Don't forget to remove the cloves before serving. Slice, serve and enjoy!

Jambalaya

Ingredients

1 cup of chopped onion
1 cup of chopped bell pepper
1 & 1/2 cups of chopped fresh tomato
3 minced cloves garlic
1 cup chopped celery
1 tablespoon vegan butter
1 tablespoon Better Than Bouillon vegetable base
1 tablespoon garlic powder
1 tablespoon onion powder
1 teaspoon smoked paprika
1 teaspoon basil
1 teaspoon thyme
1 teaspoon cayenne pepper
3 bay leaves
1 teaspoon salt
2 cups of parboiled rice
4 cups of water
2 field sliced roast sausage

Directions

Heat a boiler over medium-high heat and add butter, onions, bell peppers, celery, and tomatoes.

Stir vegetables for about five minutes or until they sweat. Add in seasonings and bay leaves along with Better Than Bouillon and water.

Stir the ingredients and pour in the rice. Stir and reduce heat to medium-low.

Cover your pot and let simmer for 25 minutes or until rice is tender and water is absorbed. But the Jambalaya should be moist.

Next, slice and brown two roast sausages. When rice is done, add the sausage and stir. Dinner is served!

Number Of Servings:
4-6
Preparation Time:
45 minutes

Lasagna

Ingredients

Vegan Ricotta
1 cup onion
1 cup bell pepper
3 cloves of garlic minced
8oz extra firm tofu
1 & 1/2 cup vegan sour cream
1 teaspoon sea salt
1/2 teaspoon better than bouillon
1 tablespoon basil
1 teaspoon thyme
1 teaspoon crushed red pepper
5 oz spinach

Meatless Sauce
1 cup onion
3 cloves garlic minced
2 cups mushroom
1 pack of beef-less crumbles
(Beyond Beef)
6 cups of pasta sauce

1 box of lasagna pasta
2 cups of vegan cheese

Number Of Servings:
4-6
Preparation Time:
1 Hour

Directions

Preheat oven to 400ºF.

Sauce:
In a medium pot over medium heat, cook onion and garlic in oil until lightly browned. Add mushroom and beef-less crumbles and cook until heated through Add 6 cups of marinara sauce and let the sauce simmer on low heat for 30 minutes.

To make the tofu ricotta:
Add oil to a hot pan throw in the onion, garlic and bell pepper. Cook them for 5 min Crumble tofu then add to the pan mix well to combine.

Add spinach and vegan sour cream to the tofu mixture. Stir to combine.

To assemble:
Cook pasta noodles according to the package and drain well.
Spread some of the sauce reserved from that 1/2 of the jar on the bottom of a 9x13 glass casserole dish.
layer meat-less sauce, noodles, ricotta and repeat. Top with a layer of vegan cheese.

Cover with foil and bake for 45 minutes covered,
Serve and enjoy!

Mushroom Barley

Ingredients

1 cup of onion
3 cloves of garlic
8 oz mushroom
1 tablespoon vegan butter
1 teaspoon salt
1/2 teaspoon pepper
1 tablespoon thyme
2 tablespoon parsley
1 teaspoon better than bouillon
1/2 cup of white wine
1&1/2 cups barley
4 cups of water

Directions

Heat vegan butter in a saucepan

Add onion, garlic and cook 4 minutes until soft

Add mushroom, cook 5 minutes stirring occasionally

Add better than bouillon and seasoning. Pour in white wine and cook until evaporated. Add barley and water

Bring to a boil, reduce heat, cover and simmer 40 minutes until liquid evaporates stirring occasionally
If liquid evaporates before barley is cooked, more water

Once barley is soft, its ready to serve.

Number Of Servings:
4-6
Preparation Time:
45 minutes

Po Boy

Ingredients

Vegetable oil, for frying
1 8oz pack of Vegan king prawn
1 cup all-purpose flour
1 cup yellow cornmeal
2 tablespoons vegan sour cream
1 tablespoon Almond milk
1/2 tablespoon salt
1/2 teaspoon cayenne pepper
1 teaspoon thyme
1 teaspoon basil
2 teaspoons garlic powder
1 teaspoon smoked paprika
1/2 teaspoon black pepper
2 small French bread loaves, each
about 10-inches long
4 tablespoons melted vegan butter
(earth balance)
1/4 cup vegan mayo
1 cup shredded lettuce
1 dill pickle sliced thin

Number Of Servings:
2
Preparation Time:
30 minutes

Directions

Heat the oil in a large sauce pan or preheat a deep fryer to 360 degrees F.

In a medium-mixing bowl, combine the flour and cornmeal. Add seasoning.

Take sour cream and milk and mix them together.

Dredge vegan prawns into sour cream mixture and then dredge vegan prawns in the seasoned flour mixture, coating them completely.

Fry the vegan prawns in the hot oil, until golden brown, stirring constantly, about 3 minutes. Remove from the oil and drain on a paper-lined plate.

Split the French bread loaves in half and brush both cut sides of the bread with some of the melted butter.Toast in toaster oven 2-3 minutes just enough to warm bread.

Using a spatula spread the vegan mayo on both sides of the bread.Divide the shrimp evenly between the 2 sandwiches. Garnish with lettuce and sliced pickles. (Hot sauce is a nice add if desired.)

Portobello Burgers

Ingredients

4 Portobello mushroom caps,
gills removed
2 tablespoons olive oil
1/2 teaspoon salt
1/2 teaspoon basil
1/4 teaspoon freshly ground
black pepper
1 small avocado, peeled, pitted
and thinly sliced
1/2 cup roasted red peppers,
thinly sliced
Toppings
1/4 cup vegan mayo
1/2 cup saluted Onions
1 cup baby spinach
4 vegan hamburger buns
8 thin slices of tomato

Number Of Servings:
4
Preparation Time:
45 minutes

Directions

Preheat a grill to medium-high.

Drizzle the olive oil on both sides
of the mushroom caps and
season with the basil salt and
pepper. Transfer the mushrooms
to the grill and cook for 4 to 5
minutes per side, or until tender.

Assemble the burgers by
spreading the Mayo on the
bottom half of the buns. Arrange
one quarter of the avocado slices
on each bottom bun and then
add the roasted red peppers and.
Place the mushroom caps on top
of the olives. Add the saluted
onions on top of each
mushroom. Arrange 1/4 cup of
the baby spinach on top of the
saluted onions top with 2 slices.
Place the bun tops on each
burger. Serve.

Pot Pie Braided Crescent

Ingredients

1 cup carrots

1 cup celery

1 cup onion

1 cup potatoes

1 cup peas

1 teaspoon vegan butter

1 teaspoon garlic powder

1 teaspoon smoked paprika

1 teaspoon basil

1 teaspoon thyme

1 Tablespoon arrowroot powder

1-1/2 teaspoon salt

1/2 teaspoon cayenne pepper

1 teaspoon better than bouillon
vegetable base

1-1/2 cashew milk

1 cup of mock chick'n

2 puff pastry dough sheets

Directions

In a large saucepan, melt the vegan butter. Add onions and saute until tender and translucent.
Stir in arrowroot powder, and allow to heat for about 2 minutes, until it changes to a golden color.

Add better than bouillon vegetable base and vegan milk, stirring constantly to avoid lumps.
Stir in chopped vegetables, and seasonings. cook for 15 min remove from heat and set aside.
On a large, greased cookie sheet (or 2, depending on how large your sheet is), unroll your crescent rolls, leaving them all attached.

Pinch together the seams of the pastry dough. Then flip it over and pinch the seams on the other side. You can either connect the two crescent rolls together to make one long pot pie crescent braid or leave them separate for two smaller.

Leaving about 3 inches in the middle of the dough, cut 1-inch thick strips down the sides of the pastry dough. Use a pizza cutter for this part.Spread the mixture down the center of the crescent dough.

Take the first strip on one side of the crescent dough and fold it over to the center of the filling. Do the same on the other side. Continue with the pattern until all strips are folded over the filling and form a braid-like pattern.
With a pastry brush, lightly brush vegan milk the top of the crescent braid.

Bake in a 400° oven for 30-35 minutes until crescent braid is golden and cooked through.
Allow Pot Pie Crescent Braid to stand for at least 10 minutes before cutting.
Serve warm.

Number Of Servings:
4
Preparation Time:
45 minutes

Vegan Red Beans & Rice

Ingredients

1 pound dried "light red" kidney beans (Camellia)

1 tablespoons vegan butter

1 teaspoon Better Than Bouillon Veggie Base

1 cup onions

1/2 cup celery

3 cloves chopped garlic

1 cup bell pepper

1 teaspoon salt

1/2 teaspoon cayenne

1 tablespoon basil

1 teaspoon smoked paprika

1 tablespoons thyme

1 tablespoon onion powder

3 bay leaves

2 field roast sausage

10 cups water

Number Of Servings:
4
Preparation Time:
45 minutes

Directions

In a large pot, heat the vegan butter over medium-high heat. Chop and add the onions, celery, garlic and bell peppers to the butter in the pot.

Then, add salt, pepper & cayenne to cook, stirring, until the vegetables are soft. This should only take 4 minutes. Add the bay leaves, parsley, thyme, paprika, basil, and garlic. Cook another 4 minutes and then add beans, Better Than Bouillon, and water. Stir and bring to a boil.

Reduce the heat to medium-low, let simmer uncovered, stirring occasionally. In about 3 hours, the beans should be tender and start to thicken. (Should the liquid covering the beans become too thick and dry, simply add 1/4 cup more water at a time.)

Just before the beans are done, start a pot of rice. Let your water come to a complete boil before adding in. Stir and cover.

while rice cooks, slice the field roast sausages into small pieces and fry till crispy on both sides.
The bean juice should be thick and gravy like, if you want the gravy to thicken reduce heat and cook beans until they are the desired constancy the beans should be tender to touch. If not, allow them to cook longer. Only when you're sure they're done, stir the pan-fried sausages into the beans. Remove from heat and take out the bay leaves as well. Serve the red

Vegan Shrimp & Grits

Ingredients
Shrimp
1 pack of vegan king prawn
2 tablespoons vegetable oil
1/4 cup all-purpose flour
1 medium onion, finely chopped
1/2 cup celery chopped
1 medium-size green bell pepper, chopped
2 garlic cloves, chopped
1/3 cup barbecue sauce
1 bay leaf
1/4 teaspoon cayenne pepper
1 teaspoon smoked paprika
1 teaspoon thyme
1/4 teaspoon black pepper
1 teaspoon garlic powder
1 teaspoon onion powder
1 teaspoon basil
Pinch of kelp powder
1 cup vegetable broth
Grits
2 1/2 cups water
1 teaspoon salt
1 1/2 cups uncooked stone ground grits
2 tablespoons vegan butter (earth balance)
1 cup vegan cheese

Number Of Servings:
4
Preparation Time:
45 minutes

Directions
Heat oil in a Dutch oven over medium heat; stir in flour, and cook, stirring constantly until flour is caramel colored (takes about 8 to 10 minutes).

Add onion, garlic, bell pepper, barbecue sauce, bay leaf and celery. Cook, stirring often, 5 to 7 minutes or until tender.
Add vegetable broth with kelp powder and remaining seasoning.

Reduce heat to low, and cook, stirring occasionally, 20 minutes.

Add vegan king prawn shrimp, and cook 10 minutes, stir until sauce has reached desired consistency.

Meanwhile, bring water and salt to a boil in a saucepan over high heat. Gradually stir in grits. Reduce heat to low, and simmer, stirring occasionally, 30 to 35 minutes or until thickened.

Add butter, cheese, and pepper. Remove bay leaves. Serve Creole Shrimp over grits.

SIDE DISHES

Ingredients

1 tablespoon vegan butter
1 large yellow onion, dice
3 garlic cloves minced
1 bell pepper, medium dice
1 celery stalk, medium dice
4 cups shelled black-eyed peas,
crowder peas
1 quart water
1 teaspoon smoked paprika
1 tablespoon better than bouillon
2 teaspoons salt
1 teaspoon thyme
1/2 teaspoon freshly ground
black pepper
1 bay leaf.

Directions

in a medium pot add the onion, garlic, bell pepper, celeryandvegan butter.Cookover medium heat until tender, about 4 to 5 minutes.

Add the water, peas, bouillon, thyme, paprika, salt, pepper and bay leaf and cook over medium heat, partially covered until the peas are tender, stir often to prevent peas from sticking about 1 hour. Add more water if necessary.

black-eyed peas are delicious served over rice.

Number Of Servings:
4-6
Preparation Time:
1 Hour and 15 minutes

Ingredients

1 cup chopped onions
1/4 cup bell peppers
2 cloves of garlic
1/4 cup smoked sun dried tomatoes
1 tablespoon garlic powder
1 tablespoon onion powder
2 teaspoon salt (add to taste)
1 teaspoon black pepper
1/4 teaspoon cayenne
1 teaspoon crushed red pepper
1 teaspoon basil
1 teaspoon smoked paprika
1 teaspoon thyme
1/4 cup vegan butter (earth balance)
1 tablespoon better than bouillon
6 cups water
3 pounds of greens (mustard greens, collard greens or turnip greens) (cleaned and stemmed)

Directions

In a large pot and add butter, garlic, onions, and bell peppers. Allow these ingredients to cook for about 6 to 7 minutes or until the onions arebrown and translucent.

Next, add all of the Cajun seasonings listed above into the pot.

Add the better than bouillon vegetable base and sun dried tomatoes and let cook for a couple of minutes.

Begin adding the greens, a third at a time, pressing down on the greens as they wilt. They will wilt considerable as they cook. Cook, uncovered, over medium heat, stirring often. The greens should cook for about 2 hours 30 minutes or until tender.

Number Of Servings:
6-8
Preparation Time:
3 Hours

Ingredients

8 ears of corn
2 tablespoons vegan butter
1 cup coconut milk
1/4 cup flour
1/3 cup red onion
1 teaspoon sea salt
1 teaspoon black pepper
1 teaspoon smoked paprika
1 tablespoon sugar

Directions

In a large bowl, cut the tip off cob. Cut the kernels from cob with a small paring knife. Using the back of the blade, scrape against the cob to press out the milky liquid.

Whisk together sugar, flour, salt, pepper and paprika in a bowl along with the corn. Add the coconut cream. Mix.

In a large cast iron skillet over high heat, heat vegan butter then add onions. Salute onions 5 minutes, until browned. Add corn mixture and turn heat down to medium-high, stirring until it becomes tender, about 30 minutes.

Number Of Servings:
6-8
Preparation Time:
3 Hours

Ingredients

12oz macaroni pasta
4oz tofu extra firm or steamed cauliflower if your soy sensitive
1 tablespoon vegan butter (earth balance)
1/2 cup onion
1/2 cup bell pepper
1 cup milk alternative
1 tablespoon flour
1 cup vegan sour cream (tofutti)
2 teaspoon smoked paprika
1 teaspoon basil
1 teaspoon thyme
1 tablespoon onion powder
1 tablespoon garlic powder
2 teaspoon salt
1/2 teaspoon red pepper flakes
1 bag vegan cheddar cheese (So delicious)
1 tablespoon Better Than Bouillon Vegetable Base

Directions

Preheat your oven to 400° degrees FH start cooking your pasta as per instructions on the box.

In a pan, melt 1 tablespoon of vegan butter, then add the onions and bell peppers. Sauté ingredients for roughly 10 minutes till onions are brown and translucent.

In a blender, add the onions, bell peppers, vegan milk, flour, sour cream, Better Than Bouillon, tofu, vegan cheese and seasonings.

Blend the cheese mixture for 3 minutes till everything is smooth.

Pour the cheese into a pot and allow it to heat for 5 minutes.

Place your pasta in a casserole dish, then cover the pasta with the cheese mix, stirring to make sure all the pasta is covered.

Place the pan in the oven to bake and remove after 30 minutes.

Number Of Servings:
6-8
Preparation Time:
1 Hours

Ingredients

Ingredients:
1/2 cup vegan butter
2 teaspoon ground cinnamon
1 cup granulated sugar
1/4 cup brown sugar
1 tablespoon pure vanilla extract.
6 medium sweet potatoes

Directions

Preheat the oven to 350 F.
Wash, Peel, then slice the yams (make sure that they are about 1/2 inch thick.)

Transfer the yams into a 9x13 dish.
Place the butter into a medium sized pot, then melt it over medium heat.

Once the butter is melted, sprinkle in the sugar, ground cinnamon.Turn the stove off, mix the ingredients, then add in the vanilla extract.

Pour the candied mixture over the yams, and try to coat all the yams with the candied mixture.

Next, cover dish, then bake the yams in the oven for 2 hours.

Remove the yams from the oven, and let them sit for about 10 minutes before serving.
Enjoy!

Number Of Servings:
6-8
Preparation Time:
2 Hours

SMOOTHIES

Boost Smoothie

Ingredients

1 orange
1 large carrot, chopped
1 cup frozen mango chunks
1/2 cup kale
1/4 cup coconut water
1 teaspoon ginger
1 teaspoon turmeric
1/4 teaspoon cayenne pepper

Directions

Place all ingredients into a blender and process till smooth. Pour into glass, enjoy!

Go Green Smoothie

Ingredients

1 cup coconut water
1 cup raw chopped kale
1 mini cucumber, chopped
1 small green apple, cored and chopped
1 teaspoon lemon juice

Directions

Place all ingredients into a blender and blend till smooth. Make one for now and save some for later. Can be stored in a mason jar or glass with lid for up to 24 hours.

Peanut Butter Dream

Ingredients
1 teaspoon cocoa powder
2 frozen bananas
1 tablespoon peanut butter
1 cup almond milk

Directions
Place all ingredients into a blender and process till smooth. Pour into glass, enjoy!

Red Velvet Smoothie

Ingredients

4 dates
5 strawberries
1 cup almond milk
1 beet
1 tablespoon cocoa powder

Directions

Place all ingredients into a blender and blend till smooth.

Strawberry Mango Smoothie

Ingredients

5 frozen strawberries
1 cup frozen mango chunks
1 banana
1 cup coconut milk
1 tsp chia seed

Directions

Place all ingredients into a blender and process till smooth. Pour into glass, enjoy!

Index

Index

Made in the USA
Columbia, SC
23 November 2018